LET'S ROCK

METAMORPHIC ROCKS

CHRIS OXLADE

Heinemann
LIBRARY

Chicago, Illinois

www.capstonepub.com
Visit our website to find out more information about Heinemann-Raintree books.

To order:
☎ Phone 800-747-4992
💻 Visit www.capstonepub.com
to browse our catalog and order online.

Edited by Louise Galpine and Diyan Leake
Designed by Victoria Allen
Illustrated by KJA artists
Picture research by Hannah Taylor
Originated by Capstone Global Library Ltd
Printed in the United States of America in North Mankato, Minnesota. 092012 006824

14 13 12
10 9 8 7 6 5 4 3 2 1

Library of Congress Cataloging-in-Publication Data
Oxlade, Chris.
  Metamorphic rocks / Chris Oxlade.
    p. cm. — (Let's rock!)
  Includes bibliographical references and index.
  ISBN 978-1-4329-4680-7 (hb)
  ISBN 978-1-4329-4688-3 (pb)
  1. Rocks, Metamorphic—Juvenile literature. 2. Petrology—Juvenile literature. I. Title.
  QE475.A2O95 2011
  552'.4—dc22   2010022203

Acknowledgments
The author and publisher are grateful to the following for permission to reproduce copyright material: Alamy Images pp. **4** (© Linda Reinink-Smith), **14** (© Lynne Evans), **16** (© Dennis Cox), **18** (© Antony Ratcliffe), **24** (© Toby Adamson); © Capstone Publishers p. **29** (Karon Dubke); Corbis pp. **12** (Visuals Unlimited), **19** (Lee Frost/Robert Harding World Imagery); GeoScience Features Picture Library p. **10** left and right (Prof. B Booth); reproduced with the permission of Natural Resources Canada 2010, courtesy of the Geological Survey of Canada p. **15**; Photolibrary pp. **17** (Rob Jung), **20** (Superstock), **21** (Jeffery Titcomb), **22** (Robert Harding/Roy Rainford), **23** (Joe Cornish), **26** (Britain on View/ Steve Lewis); Science Photo Library pp. **5** (Gregory Dimijian), **9** (G. Brad Lewis), **11** (Dirk Wiersma).

Cover photograph of mountain peaks in the Mont Blanc range of the French Alps reproduced with permission of Photolibrary (Robert Harding Travel/Peter Richardson).

We would like to thank Dr. Stuart Robinson for his invaluable help in the preparation of this book.

Every effort has been made to contact copyright holders of any material reproduced in this book. Any omissions will be rectified in subsequent printings if notice is given to the publisher.

Disclaimer
All the Internet addresses (URLs) given in this book were valid at the time of going to press. However, due to the dynamic nature of the Internet, some addresses may have changed, or sites may have changed or ceased to exist since publication. While the author and publisher regret any inconvenience this may cause readers, no responsibility for any such changes can be accepted by either the author or the publisher.

CONTENTS

Rock roles

Find out about the work involved in the study of rocks.

Science tip

Check out our smart tips to learn more about rocks.

Number crunching

Discover the amazing numbers in the world of rocks.

Biography

Read about people who have made important discoveries in the study of rocks.

Some words are printed in bold, **like this**. You can find out what they mean by looking in the glossary on page 30.

WHAT ARE METAMORPHIC ROCKS?

Down inside Earth, many miles below the surface, hot **molten** rock forces its way upward through cracks in the solid rock nearer the surface. Heat from the molten rock flows into the solid rock, heating that rock to temperatures of hundreds of degrees—and even over a thousand degrees—Fahrenheit. The heat makes it change into a new type of rock, called metamorphic rock. The word *metamorphic* means "changing form."

MINERALS AND CRYSTALS

All rock, not just metamorphic rock, is made from materials called **minerals**. Metamorphic rocks are made from a mixture of different minerals, and sometimes just one mineral. Minerals themselves are made up of **atoms**, which are arranged in rows and columns. Materials with atoms arranged like this are called **crystals**.

This is an outcrop of **gneiss** (say "nice"), a common metamorphic rock, on the west coast of Sweden.

This is a sample of a mineral called labradorite, which is found in some metamorphic rocks. It comes in several colors, not just blue.

THREE TYPES OF ROCK

Metamorphic rock is just one type of rock. The other two types are **sedimentary rock** and **igneous rock**. Sedimentary rock is made when tiny pieces of rock, or the skeletons or shells of sea animals, are buried underground and compressed. Igneous rock is made when molten rock cools and becomes solid.

THE ROCK CYCLE

New metamorphic rock is always being formed, and it is always being destroyed. This is part of a process called the **rock cycle**. In this book we follow the journey of metamorphic rock as it moves around the rock cycle. You can see a diagram of the rock cycle on page 8.

WHAT IS INSIDE EARTH?

Earth is a giant ball of rock. If you dig a hole deep enough anywhere on Earth, you will eventually come to solid rock. This is part of the rocky outer layer that covers Earth, called the **crust**. Some of the rock is metamorphic rock. Most metamorphic rocks begin their journey inside the crust.

HOW THICK IS THE CRUST?

Under the **continents** the crust is between 25 and 90 kilometers (15 and 56 miles) thick, but under the oceans it is only between 6 and 11 kilometers (4 and 7 miles) thick. The crust sits on top of very hot rock below. This hot rock forms a layer 2,900 kilometers (1,800 miles) deep called the **mantle**.

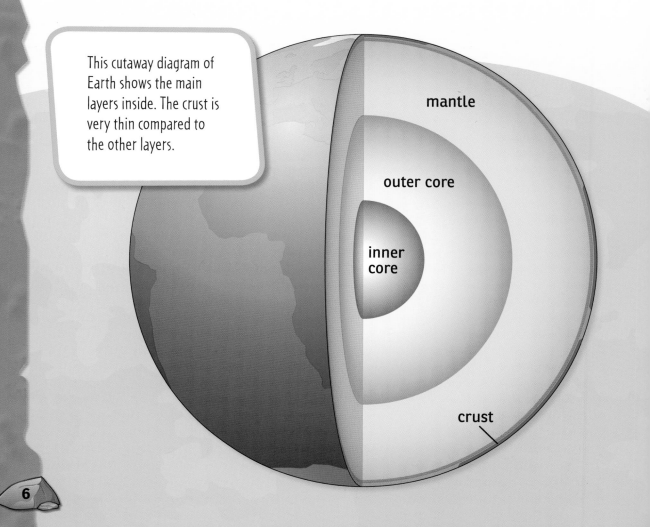

This cutaway diagram of Earth shows the main layers inside. The crust is very thin compared to the other layers.

mantle

outer core

inner core

crust

A CRACKED CRUST

The crust is cracked into many large pieces called **tectonic plates**. They move around, but only at speeds of a few inches a year. The lines where the plates meet each other are called **plate boundaries**. At some boundaries the plates move toward each other, and here rocks are destroyed and changed.

Here, two tectonic plates are moving toward each other. Their rocks are crushed by immense forces. Metamorphic rocks are often formed here.

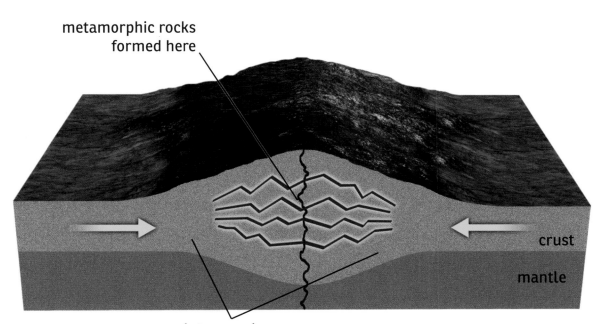

metamorphic rocks formed here

crust

mantle

plates moving toward each other

THE ROCK CYCLE

During the **rock cycle**, new rocks, including metamorphic rocks, are made all the time, and old rocks are destroyed all the time. Most metamorphic rocks are made from **sedimentary rocks** and **igneous rocks**. You can find out how sedimentary and igneous rocks are changed into metamorphic rocks on page 10.

The change that happens when a rock becomes a metamorphic rock is called **metamorphism**. Most metamorphic rock takes thousands or millions of years to form, but it can take billions of years to move through the crust before finally being destroyed.

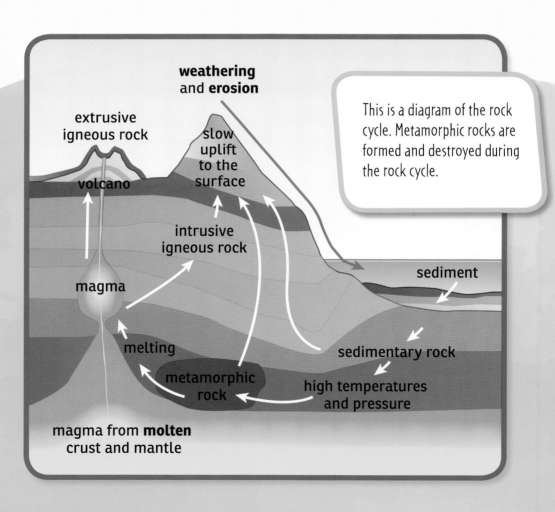

weathering and erosion

extrusive igneous rock

slow uplift to the surface

volcano

This is a diagram of the rock cycle. Metamorphic rocks are formed and destroyed during the rock cycle.

intrusive igneous rock

sediment

magma

melting

sedimentary rock

metamorphic rock

high temperatures and pressure

magma from **molten** crust and mantle

CHANGING BACK

In the rock cycle, metamorphic rocks and other rocks are also **recycled** into new rocks, which may be sedimentary or igneous rocks. Some sedimentary rocks, such as sandstone and clay, are made from **particles** (very small pieces) of other rocks joined together. Some igneous rocks are made when other rocks melt and then cool again.

Biography

Charles Lyell (1797–1875) was a Scottish scientist who traveled long distances to study rock formations in Europe, including the volcano Mount Etna in Sicily. Through his observations, he realized that Earth's surface is changing all the time. He concluded that the mountains, valleys, and other features on Earth's surface are made naturally over millions of years. At that time, most people thought that Earth was just a few thousand years old.

This is a lava flow from Kilauea, a volcano on the island of Hawaii. Some of the **minerals** in this rock may have come from metamorphic rock that has melted.

HOW ARE METAMORPHIC ROCKS MADE?

The journey of metamorphic rocks begins with other types of rock. They can be **igneous rocks**, **sedimentary rocks**, or even other metamorphic rocks. The rocks change to metamorphic rocks when they are heated, or put under immense **pressure**, or both. The rocks do not melt, but their **minerals** are destroyed and **crystals** of new minerals form. Nothing is added to the rocks as they change, and nothing is taken away. The chemicals that make up the minerals are just rearranged to make new minerals.

Shale (left) is a sedimentary rock. Under immense heat and pressure, it can become gneiss (right), a metamorphic rock.

WHERE METAMORPHIC ROCKS COME FROM

So, where are the conditions right for metamorphic rocks to be made? The answer is where there is either **magma** to provide heat, or where there is great pressure in the **crust**. Magma is produced at **destructive boundaries**, and great pressure is created in the crust at **collision boundaries**, so these are the places where most metamorphic rocks are made.

Science tip

When metamorphic rocks are made, the crystals of minerals in the rock are changed. You can see crystals of minerals in some types of rock. Look at them close up with a magnifying glass. You can easily see crystals in metamorphic rocks called **schists** and **gneisses**. Or you can examine **granite**, a common igneous rock.

This photo shows a band of speckled white, black, and blue **quartz** surrounded by slate.

METAMORPHIC ROCKS MADE BY HEAT

Some metamorphic rocks begin their journey when rocks are touched by red-hot magma in the crust. Only those rocks that are close enough to the magma to be heated will be changed. Rocks far from the magma are not changed at all. This sort of change is called **local metamorphism**. (It is also called contact metamorphism.)

Local metamorphism happens wherever magma rises into the crust. The magma might be on its way to the surface to form a **volcano**, or rising into the rocks above to form a huge bulge of new igneous rock. The bulge is called an intrusion.

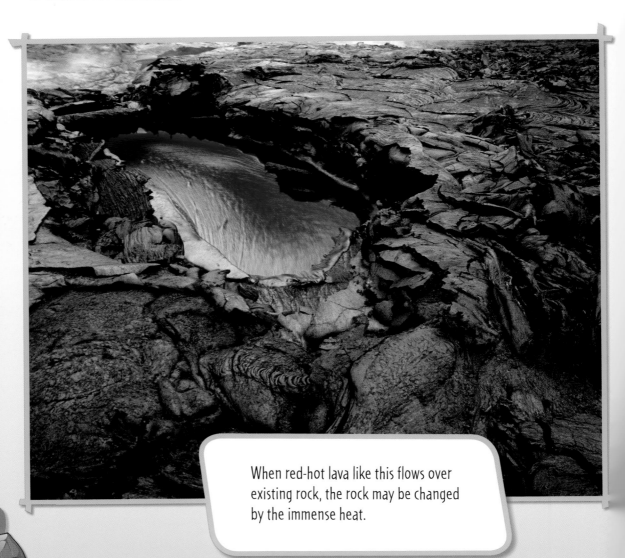

When red-hot lava like this flows over existing rock, the rock may be changed by the immense heat.

HOW HEAT CHANGES ROCKS

Magma is hot—extremely hot! It can have a temperature of 1,000 °C (1,832 °F) or more. It heats up any solid rock it touches. The rocks it touches are cooked, and their minerals change. Imagine magma flowing next to mudstone, which is a sedimentary rock. Because of the heat, new minerals form in the mudstone, creating a metamorphic rock with dark spots in it called hornfels.

Rock role

A **geologist** is a scientist who studies how rocks are made, how they change, and how they make up Earth. Some geologists study geomorphology, which is how the landscape changes. This includes studying metamorphic rocks, because the age and position of metamorphic rocks are evidence of what happened to rocks in the past.

The heat from red-hot magma flowing through sedimentary rock changes the rock to metamorphic rock.

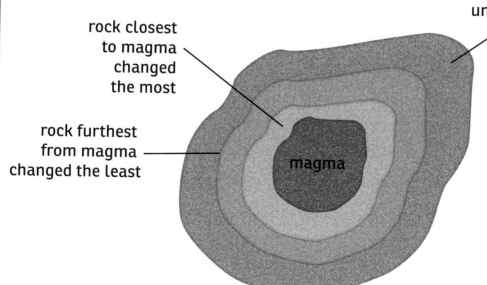

rock closest to magma changed the most

original rock unchanged

rock furthest from magma changed the least

magma

METAMORPHIC ROCKS MADE BY PRESSURE

Some metamorphic rocks begin their journeys deep in the crust, where they are formed by enormous pressure. The changes happen over a very large area—perhaps hundreds and even thousands of miles across. This sort of **metamorphism** is called **regional metamorphism**.

Regional metamorphism happens where two **tectonic plates** are moving toward each other. One of the plates sinks under the other, and the rocks in this plate are put under huge pressure as they move down toward the **mantle**. Some change into metamorphic rocks. Others get so hot that they melt, creating lots of magma that rises into the crust. This magma heats the rocks in the plate above, creating more metamorphic rocks.

There are beautiful patterns in Lewissian gneiss found in the Western Isles of Scotland. These rocks were made by regional metamorphism.

METAMORPHIC ROCKS AND MOUNTAINS

Some of the world's great mountain ranges, such as the Alps and the Himalayas, were formed when two plates crashed slowly together. In the crust under the mountains, huge pressure created metamorphic rocks. There are often huge amounts of metamorphic rocks under mountain ranges.

Number crunching

All of the world's oldest rocks are metamorphic rocks. The oldest rock found so far is a type of schist called greenstone, found in northern Canada, which is 4.3 billion years old. Earth itself is 4.5 billion years old. See page 25 to find out how geologists measure the age of rocks.

This is some of the oldest rock on Earth. It was found near the Acasta River, in Canada.

WHAT TYPES OF METAMORPHIC ROCK ARE THERE?

There are dozens of different metamorphic rocks. How a metamorphic rock looks depends on the original rock from which it was formed, and also the place where it was made. For example, shale (a **sedimentary rock**) can be turned into the metamorphic rocks slate, **schist**, or **gneiss**.

The following are some examples of metamorphic rocks:

Slate is a dark, fine-**grained** rock made when shale is put under high pressure. It splits easily into thin sheets.

Schists are medium-grained metamorphic rocks made from shale or mudstone. There are many types of schists in different colors.

Gneiss is formed at very high temperatures and pressures from different **igneous** and sedimentary rocks. It is coarse-grained and has bands of **minerals** that are often bent and folded.

Marble is formed when **limestone** is heated to very high temperatures (see page 20).

Quartzite is formed when sandstone is heated. It is mostly made from the mineral **quartz**.

This metamorphic mica schist formation is in the Namib Desert, in Africa.

Identifying metamorphic rocks

Metamorphic rocks are normally very hard, dull in appearance, and quite rough to touch. A rock with bands of color is probably gneiss. Rocks with large **crystals** in a fine-grained background are probably metamorphic, too. You can use the table here to help you identify metamorphic rock.

Rock	Color	Foliated*	Grain size
slate	dark gray	yes	fine
schist	mixture	no	medium
gneiss	pink/gray	yes	coarse
marble	light	no	coarse
quartzite	light	no	coarse

* *Foliated* means a rock has bands of minerals in it.

This is quartzite, a metamorphic rock made when sandstone is changed by heat and pressure. This example is in Kimberley, in Australia.

HOW DO WE USE METAMORPHIC ROCKS?

Metamorphic rocks are not commonly found on Earth's surface. Most of the rocks we use as materials are **sedimentary** and **igneous** rocks, which are easier to find. However, where metamorphic rocks are found, we use them for building and other jobs.

Schist and **gneiss** are tough rocks that are good for building. They are also crushed into gravel for making concrete and for paving. Some schists and gneisses have attractive **crystals** and patterns and are often used for decorative buildings and ornamental stonework.

Slate has some very useful properties. It can be easily split into flat sheets, and it is almost completely waterproof. This makes it a popular material for making roof and floor tiles. Monuments and nameplates are also made from slate because it is easy to carve.

These traditional houses in Nepal have roofs made from slate, a metamorphic rock, split into thin sheets.

METAMORPHIC ROCKS IN THE PAST

Rocks were one of the first materials that humans used. We do not know when people first used metamorphic rocks, but it may have been hundreds of thousands of years ago—possibly to make simple tools, or shelters.

These standing stones were erected thousands of years ago at Callanish, on the island of Lewis in Scotland. They are made of Lewissian gneiss.

Rock role

A sculptor is a craftsperson who shapes materials to make statues and other sculptures. The sculptor uses tools such as chisels to cut away the rock. Sculptors often work with rock because it will last for a long time. Schists, gneisses, slates, and **marbles** are all used for sculpture.

MARVELOUS MARBLE

Marble is a metamorphic rock that is formed when **limestone** is changed by high temperatures. It is made mostly from a **mineral** called **calcite** (also called calcium carbonate). Pure marble is mostly white, but marble often contains other minerals that create colors, such as black, red, and green, and beautiful patterns.

Marble is quite easy to cut and polish to make a shiny finish. That is why marble is used for decoration in buildings. It can be found on the outside of buildings and on walls and floors. Marble is also used for making ornaments and sculptures. Some other decorative rocks look like marble and are sometimes called marble, but they are not actually metamorphic rock.

This sample of Balkan Gray marble has beautiful gray and pink patterns. The white lines are called veins.

The calcite that becomes marble is an important raw material in industry. It is used in making things from paper to toothpaste. Lime, a material used to make cement, is made by heating calcite.

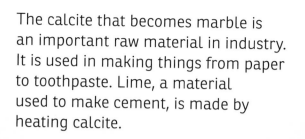

The famous statue of the biblical hero David by the Italian artist Michelangelo is carved from Carrara marble.

DO METAMORPHIC ROCKS LAST FOREVER?

How long do metamorphic rocks last before their journey ends? It is normally a very, very long time! A metamorphic rock such as a **gneiss**, made many miles down in Earth's **crust**, will last for many millions of years. Some metamorphic rocks are billions of years old. But metamorphic rocks do not last forever. Their journey eventually comes to an end.

DESTRUCTION AT EARTH'S SURFACE

Sometimes metamorphic rocks that are made deep in the crust end up at Earth's surface. Then the rocks are worn away by processes called **weathering** and **erosion**.

The jagged peaks of the Mont Blanc range in the French Alps show how ice breaks up solid rock.

Weathering is the way rocks are broken up by the action of weather. For example, in very cold places, water freezes inside cracks in the rocks and helps to break them up. Flowing water, wind, and gravity carry the broken pieces of rock away.

Flowing water and glaciers (huge masses of ice that travel down valleys) also break up the rocks they flow over. But metamorphic rocks are tough, and they wear away very slowly.

Science tip

On a trip to coastal areas, or to hills or mountains, you can see how rocks are worn away. At coastal areas, look for how cliffs are broken up by the waves—there will be broken rocks around their bases. Near hills and mountains, look for loose and broken rocks and see how the broken pieces are carried downhill by streams.

The regular movement of ocean waves causes erosion at the base of sea cliffs.

DESTRUCTION UNDERGROUND

Metamorphic rocks are destroyed where two **tectonic plates** are moving toward each other. If part of the plate sinks down into the crust or comes under pressure, any metamorphic rocks inside it are heated up and melted. The **molten** rock (**magma**) from them can rise up into the crust, cool down, and so form new **igneous rocks**.

It is not just igneous and **sedimentary rocks** that are changed into metamorphic rocks. Metamorphic rocks themselves can be changed into other metamorphic rocks. For example, a rock such as a **schist** made by **regional metamorphism** could be changed into a new form of rock by **local metamorphism**.

In the distant future, this gneiss in Scotland could be turned into another sort of metamorphic rock.

MEASURING THE AGE OF ROCKS

Geologists often need to find out how old rocks are. For example, the age of a piece of schist might them tell them when an ancient mountain range was formed. The main way of dating metamorphic rock is by radiometric dating. This method relies on the fact that, over time, some types of **atoms** change into other types (a process called radioactive decay). The amount of various types of atom in a sample is measured to figure out the age.

GEOLOGICAL TIMELINE

The age of metamorphic rocks is measured in millions of years. Age is also given by the name of the period in time when it was made. For example, a Devonian rock was made between 359 and 416 million years ago.

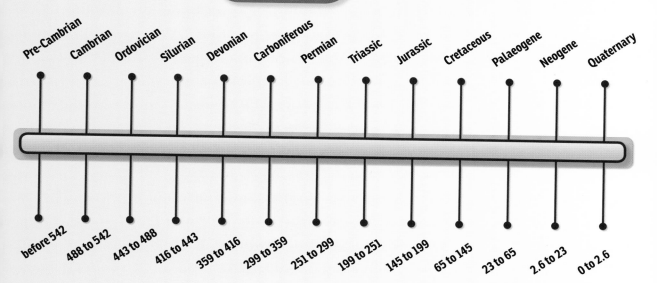

Period

Pre-Cambrian	Cambrian	Ordovician	Silurian	Devonian	Carboniferous	Permian	Triassic	Jurassic	Cretaceous	Palaeogene	Neogene	Quaternary
before 542	488 to 542	443 to 488	416 to 443	359 to 416	299 to 359	251 to 299	199 to 251	145 to 199	65 to 145	23 to 65	2.6 to 23	0 to 2.6

Dates (millions of years ago)

ARE WE HARMING METAMORPHIC ROCKS?

Metamorphic rocks such as **marble** and slate are an important resource for us. But we destroy these rocks when we take them from the ground. Rocks are dug out at **quarries**. Lots of energy is needed to dig out rocks and transport them, and digging them out creates noise and pollution. Quarrying destroys natural **habitats** for wildlife—although disused, flooded quarries often make good habitats for birds.

Rocks are destroyed and **recycled** in the **rock cycle** on a massive scale in the **crust** many miles down. Quarrying on the surface has very little effect on the rock cycle. However, we should try not to damage natural rocks, because they are part of our environment.

This disused quarry in Wales has become a river habitat for wildlife.

JOURNEY'S END

Our journey of metamorphic rock has come to its end. The journey began inside Earth's crust, where rocks were changed by extreme heat and immense pressure to make metamorphic rocks. The heat came from **molten** rock moving into the crust, and the pressure came from **tectonic plates** crushing into each other.

During the rock cycle, new metamorphic rocks are being made all the time, and old metamorphic rocks are being destroyed all the time. The rock cycle has been going on since Earth was made 4.5 billion years ago, and it will continue for billions of years to come.

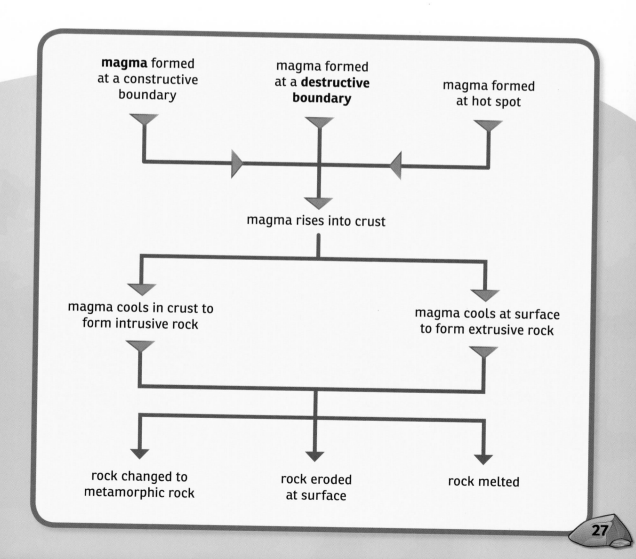

MAKE CLAY AND CHOCOLATE ROCKS!

Here's a simple experiment that will help you to understand the journey of metamorphic rocks that we have followed through this book. Before you try the experiment, read the instructions, prepare the materials you need, and find an area where you can work.

Ask an adult to help you with this experiment.

YOU WILL NEED:
- modeling clay
- chocolate
- aluminum foil
- a heavy book
- a plate
- a knife
- a microwave oven.

WHAT TO DO:

1. Break the chocolate into small pieces less than 1 centimeter (half an inch) across.

2. Take a lump of modeling clay about 6-7 centimeters (2-3 inches) across. Push the chocolate pieces into it and roll it into a ball.

3. Put the ball on the plate and put it into a microwave oven. Warm it on low power for about two minutes.

4. Put a piece of aluminum foil over the ball and put a heavy book on top of the foil. Wait for a few minutes.

5 Cut the crushed ball in half—carefully, since it might still be hot.

What do you see inside the ball? Did you get layered patterns? The heat and pressure you applied changed the structure of the clay and chocolate mixture, just as heat and pressure change **sedimentary** and **igneous rocks** into metamorphic rocks.

GLOSSARY

atom smallest particle of chemical matter that can exist

calcite type of mineral found in limestone rock

collision boundary boundary where two tectonic plates come together, creating immense pressure

continent one of the large landmasses of Earth, such as Europe, Africa, or Asia

core central part of Earth

crust rocky surface layer of Earth

crystal shape a mineral grows into as a result of the neat rows and columns of atoms

destructive boundary boundary between two tectonic plates where rocks in the plates are destroyed

erosion wearing away of rocks by flowing water, wind, and glaciers

geologist scientist who studies the rocks and soil from which Earth is made

gneiss common coarse-grained metamorphic rock

grain pattern of particles in a rock (the particles can be crystals or small pieces of rock)

granite common intrusive igneous rock

habitat place where an animal or plant lives

igneous rock rock formed when magma (molten rock) cools and solidifies

limestone common sedimentary rock made up of the mineral calcite, which can come from the shells and skeletons of sea animals

local metamorphism when metamorphic rocks are made over a small area (up to a few miles across), normally by contact with hot magma

magma molten rock below Earth's crust

mantle very deep layer of hot rock below Earth's crust

marble metamorphic rock made from the sedimentary rock limestone

metamorphism change that happens when rock becomes metamorphic rock

mineral substance that is naturally present in Earth, such as gold and salt

molten melted

particle small piece of material

plate boundary place where one tectonic plate meets another

pressure force or weight pressing against something

quarry place where large amounts of rock are dug out of the ground

quartz hard mineral, often found in crystal form

recycle process of changing something into something new

regional metamorphism when metamorphic rocks are made over a large area (perhaps hundreds or even thousands of miles across), normally by pressure in the crust

rock cycle constant formation, destruction, and recycling of rocks through Earth's crust

schist common medium-grained metamorphic rock

sedimentary rock rock made when tiny pieces of rock or the skeletons or shells of sea animals are buried underground and compressed

tectonic plate one of the giant pieces that Earth's crust is cracked into

volcano opening in Earth's surface where magma escapes from underground

weathering breaking up of rocks by weather conditions such as extremes of temperature

FIND OUT MORE

BOOKS

Faulkner, Rebecca. *Metamorphic Rock* (Geology Rocks!). Chicago: Raintree, 2008.

Pipe, Jim. *Earth's Rocks and Fossils* (Planet Earth). Pleasantville, N.Y.: Gareth Stevens, 2008.

Walker, Sally M. *Rocks* (Early Bird Earth Science). Minneapolis: Lerner, 2007.

WEBSITES

See animations of how rocks are formed at this website of the Franklin Institute:
www.fi.edu/fellows/fellow1/oct98/create

Find lots of information about rocks and minerals, as well as links to other interesting websites, at this site:
www.rocksforkids.com

PLACES TO VISIT

American Museum of Natural History
Central Park West at 79th Street
New York, New York, 10024-5192
Tel: (212) 769-5100
www.amnh.org
Visit a large and fascinating collection of rocks, minerals, and fossils.

The Field Museum
1400 S. Lake Shore Drive
Chicago, Illinois 60605-2496
Tel: (312) 922-9410
www.fieldmuseum.org
See fascinating exhibits of rocks, minerals, and fossils from around the world.

INDEX